369 Manifestation Journal

A 96-Day Guided Workbook to Harness the Power of The Universe

Layla Moon

Image Designed by

Freepik

Vecteezy

PUBLISHED BY: Layla Moon

© Copyright 2022 - All rights reserved.

The content contained within this book may not be reproduced, duplicated, or transmitted without direct written permission from the author or the publisher.

Under no circumstances will any blame or legal responsibility be held against the publisher, or author, for any damages, reparation, or monetary loss due to the information contained within this book, either directly or indirectly.

Legal Notice:

This book is copyright protected. It is only for personal use. You cannot amend, distribute, sell, use, quote or paraphrase any part, or the content within this book, without the consent of the author or publisher.

Disclaimer Notice:

Please note the information contained within this document is for educational and entertainment purposes only. All effort has been executed to present accurate, up to date, reliable, complete information. No warranties of any kind are declared or implied. Readers acknowledge that the author is not engaged in the rendering of legal, financial, medical, or professional advice. The content within this book has been derived from various sources. Please consult a licensed professional before attempting any techniques outlined in this book.

By reading this document, the reader agrees that under no circumstances is the author responsible for any losses, direct or indirect, that are incurred as a result of the use of the information contained within this document, including, but not limited to, errors, omissions, or inaccuracies.

Table of Contents

4 FREE Gifts	1
Chapter 1: Introduction	6
Chapter 2: What is 369?	9
The Basis of The 369 Method	11
Understanding Vortex Math	12
The Numbers of 3, 6, and 9	17
How Does the 369 Method Work?	18
Chapter 3: Tuning into the Infinite	21
Chapter 4: Affirmation and Manifestation	31
Chapter 5: Self-Care and Manifestation	38
Chapter 6: Journaling Guide	41
Step #1 - Setting Up Your Workbook	42
Step #2 - The 369 Method	42
Step #3 - Live the 96 Days!	45
Conclusion	46

PART TWO: JOURNAL	**48**
Day 1 – 10: Building Your Self-Confidence	51
Day 11 – 20: Manifesting Love, Romance, and Relationships	73
Day 21 – 30: Creating abundance in all areas of life	95
Day 31 – 40: Improving Your Health and Well-Being	117
Day 41 – 50: Developing Your Creativity	139
Day 51 – 60: Achieving Your Goals and Dreams	161
Day 61 – 70: Manifesting Your Ideal Career or Job	181
Day 71 – 80: Creating a Life You Love	201
Day 81 – 90: Forgiving Yourself and Others	223
Day 91 - 96 - Manifest Your Reality	245

4 FREE Gifts

To help you along your spiritual journey, I've created 4 FREE bonus eBooks.

You can get instant access by signing up to my email newsletter below. On top of the 4 free books, you will also receive weekly tips along with free book giveaways, discounts, and so much more.

All of these bonuses are 100% free with no strings attached. You don't need to provide any personal information except your email address.

To get your bonus, go to:

https://dreamlifepress.com/four-free-gifts

Or scan the QR code below

Spirit Guides for Beginners: How to Hear the Universe's Call and Communicate with Your Spirit Guide and Guardian Angels

Guided by Moon herself, inspired by her own experiences and knowledge that has been passed down by hundreds of generations for thousands of years, you'll discover everything you need to know to;

- Understanding what the call of the universe is
- How to hear and comprehend it
- Knowing who and what your spirit guides and guardian angels are
- Learning how to connect, start a conversation, and listen to your guides
- How to manifest your dreams with the help of the cosmic source
- Learning how to start living the life you want to live
- And so much more…

Law of Attraction: Manifest Your Desire

Learn how to tap into the infinite power of the universe and manifest everything you want in life.

Includes:

- Law of Attraction: Manifest Your Desire ebook
- Law of Attraction Workbook
- Cheat sheets and checklists so make sure you're on the right path

Hoodoo Book of Spells for Beginners: Easy and effective Rootwork, Conjuring, and Protection Spells for Healing and Prosperity

Harness the power of one of the greatest magics. Hoodoo is a powerful force ideal for holding negativity at bay, promoting positivity in all areas in your life, offering protection to the things you love, and ultimately taking control of your destiny.

Inside, you will discover:

- How to get started with Hoodoo in your day-to-day life
- How to use conjuration spells to manifest the life you want to live
- How casting protection spells can help you withstand the toughest of times
- Break cycles of bad luck and promote good fortune throughout your life
- Hoodoo to encourage prosperity and financial stability
- How to heal using Hoodoo magic, both short-term and long-term traumas and troubles
- Remove curses and banish pain, suffering, and negativity from your life
- And so much more…

Book of Shadows

A printable PDF to support you in your spiritual transformation.

Within the pages, you will find:
- Potion and tinctures tracking sheet
- Essential oils log pages
- Herbs log pages
- Magical rituals and spiritual body goals checklist
- Tarot reading spread sheets
- Weekly moon and planetary cycle tracker
- And so much more

Get all the resources for FREE by visiting the link below

https://dreamlifepress.com/four-free-gifts

Chapter 1

Introduction

You're about to embark on a 96-day journey that will change your life.

It's lovely to meet you. My name is Layla Moon, and I'll be your guide for the change you're about to undergo. Throughout the following pages, you'll have first-hand experience with your innate and potent ability to tap into the power of the universe and manifest the life of your dreams.

To manifest the life of your dreams means to bring into existence what you desire most. It's the ability to create your reality through the power of your thoughts, emotions, and actions.

You may be wondering how manifestation works and whether it's even real. I assure you, it is very real and has worked wonders in my life. Over the last ten years, since I started my journey into connecting with the universal power, I've been able to travel the world, manifest my dream home and car, and create a business doing what I love. My relationships have flourished, and I've managed to heal many of the past traumas that kept me trapped in toxic relationships, dangerous thought patterns, and my own self-doubt.

Of course, I'm not talking about closing your eyes and wishing for a million dollars and having it appear under your bed. I'm talking about real-time, long-lasting, sustainable changes that you bring into existence through the power of your thoughts, emotions, and actions.

This was all made possible through the Law of Attraction's 369 Method.

The 369 Method is a powerful manifestation tool that enables you to connect with the universal energy surrounding us and tap into its limitless power. The 369 Method is based on the Law of Attraction, but we'll explore the details of this together shortly.

This is all made possible through the power of journaling. Now, I know you've heard about journaling before. We all know or at least have some idea about the benefits this daily practice can bring into our lives, whether through organizing our minds or gaining clarity on what's going on, but it can be so much more.

Instead of brain-dumping your day or simply venting about the things you're going through, the 369 Method takes the practice to a whole new level. It's essentially upgrading your journaling practice from writing whatever comes to mind to giving it purpose and direction and amplifying your ability to send out the energy you want into the universe.

All of this comes together to create a manifestation process you've never seen before.

If you doubt manifestation's power or you've tried it before without success, or if you're just starting out and you're looking for guidance on how to bring this manifestation process into your own life, this book is for you.

Yes, I'm sure you have questions, and I assure you they'll be answered throughout this workbook.

For now, I want you to recognize that some part of your life has been searching for an answer. This could have been for the past few weeks, months, or years. You've put the energy of your search out into the universe, and now an actionable, powerful solution has been placed in your hands. Take a moment to breathe and let that fact wash over you.

Your solution is here.

Chapter 2

What is 369?

When The 369 Method first came to me, I was curious. It's not a practice you see every day, not like mindfulness meditation, using the Law of Attraction, or spending time in nature. So, I looked into it and was very surprised by what I found.

Read into The 369 Method to any degree, and you'll find the name 'Nikola Tesla.' That's right, the famous American inventor Nikola Tesla that most of us have heard of. He's responsible for bringing us technologies we now take for granted, like alternating current (AC) electricity and radio transmissions. Without him, our world would look and function very differently.

But what does he have to do with manifestation?

In short, Nikola Tesla was a believer in the power of manifestation. To many, he's become somewhat of a patron saint for modern-day manifestors, and for good reason. He wrote about it, talked about it, and even created the technology he's famous for based on this belief system. In his own words:

"If you want to find the secrets of the Universe, think in terms of energy, frequency, and vibration."

Nikola Tesla believed this, and his success alone proves its possible. He believed that we could use our thoughts and emotions to tap into the universal energy and create the life we desire, and it should be no surprise that you can too.

In other words, Nikola Tesla believed that everything in the universe is made up of energy vibrating at different frequencies. And he believed that we could use our thoughts and emotions to tap into this universal energy and create the life we desire.

This, at its core, is the Law of Attraction.

To manifest the life you want, you must tune into the vibrational frequencies of what you want (made possible through your manifestation practices), send them out into the universe, and the universe will send them back. Thus, you manifest your reality.

For example, if you want to attract more money into your life, you need to raise your vibration to match the frequency of more money.

You can do this by thinking and speaking positively about money, surrounding yourself with images of wealth, and taking actions that align with your financial goals.

But with all this, where does the 369 Method come in? And why the numbers 3, 6, and 9? What's so important about them?

The Basis of The 369 Method

Numbers carry power, and everything revolves around numbers. You've perhaps heard, even briefly, that math is the language of the universe. This is the foundation of numerology - the idea is that every number carries its own vibrations and has its own 'personality.'

Numbers have their own meaning. 3, 6, and 9, are the numbers of manifestation and promote a positive connection to the universe and its energy.

The angel number 369 is by far one of the most incredible positive angel numbers you can come across. It signifies completion, wholeness, and unity. Interestingly, it also represents positive change and progress in your life, which clearly signifies that beautiful things, the reality that you want to be living, are on their way.

This number is a reminder to stay motivated and encouraged. If it ever comes up in a reading, it's a sign to continue working on your life's path, seek out your soul's mission, and aim to fulfill it in your lifetime. After all, what else is life for?

However, breaking the numbers down into their individual components gives us even more insights into what they're capable of bringing into our lives and highlights why the 369 Method can do what it does.

Three is perhaps the most important. One of the most significant numbers in numerology, three is the number of manifestations. Pythagoras, the Ancient Greek philosopher, credited with the Pythagorean theorem, is known for defining number three in this way. He is celebrated for dedicating much of his life to understanding the universal power of numbers, and his work is still incredibly relevant to this day.

According to Pythagoras' theory (this one, not the triangle one), three is 'the noblest of all digits.' The number six is the number for harmony, which is essential for accurate and powerful manifestations, and nine represents the completion of a cycle. This clearly ties into manifestation and the Law of Attraction, referring to the cycle of sending energy out and having it come back to you.

This is what many call 'Vortex Math.'

Understanding Vortex Math

On the surface, vortex math is a system. It's a system that explains what form or matter is. This refers to everything in the universe. Literally anything you can imagine, from material to the stuff we can't see. When plotting this system on paper, it becomes a vortex shape. How do you plot the system?

Well, you do so using numbers, placing the Vedic numbers (the numbers one to nine) in a circle around the number zero. It looks a little something like this.

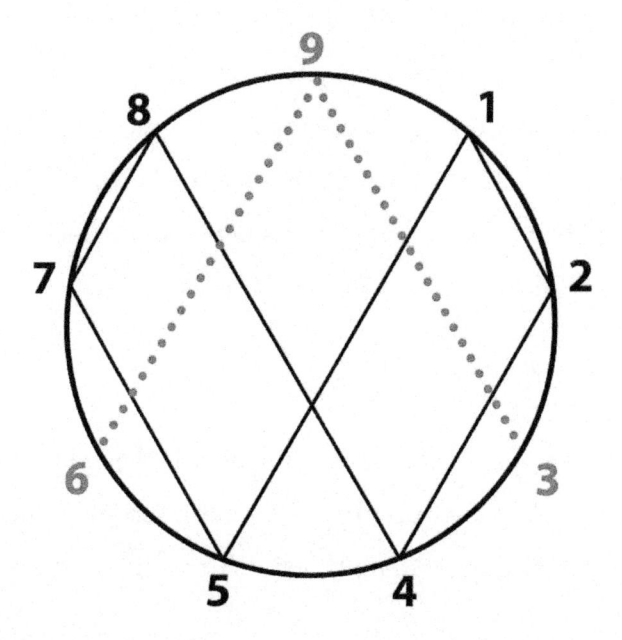

Many people believe that this is the way to reach closer to the very depth behind creation and consciousness. This is very complicated stuff, and while I'm going to do my best to explain it in the simplest way possible, there is a lot to unpack here, so feel free to skip ahead if you're not interested or do your own research to find out more if you want to go deeper.

The idea was founded and popularized by Marko Rodin, who described vortex math as a blueprint for the universe.

Vortex math basically describes the quality of the numbers that we know to be math, rather than looking into the numbers and their values at face value. It expresses how everything in our universe, from the material to the ether to the zero point, is connected.

Many believe that math wasn't invented by humans but merely discovered by them. This shows how time and time again, math has been able to prove the connections between all kinds of sciences, patterns, and inner workings. Everything, from the tiniest atom to the largest supernova or black hole, can be explained by math. It's the only constant, and being able to tap into this power can unlock a huge shift in perspective for us all.

So, how does it all work?

Well, the most important thing to remember is that all numbers have patterns, and it's these patterns that make up the universe and everything we know. For example, let's start with 1 to create a single-digit pattern.

1 multiplied by 2 is 2. 2 times 2 is 4. 4 times 2 is 8. 8 times 2 is 16, and remember, we only want single digits, so we'll add one and six together to get 7.

7 times 2 is 14, added together is 5. 5 multiplied by 2 is 10 and add these digits together, and we're back to 1.

If you're to plot these numbers around in a circle (which is known as plotting around the zero point) and link them up, linking them would create a vortex shape, which could be put onto a torus.

Now, this is important. Taking that image from the beginning of the chapter, if you put all the single-digit numbers (1-9) and plotted them evenly spaced around the circle at equal distances and draw a number from its single-digit number double (such as 2 to 4 and 4 to 8), you'll get another vortex pattern that can be placed on the surface of a torus.

But, why all this talk about the torus shape?

Well, atoms, the very structure at the heart of everything in the universe, are shaped like a torus. This is known as the toroidal ring model, originally known as Parson magneton, or a magnetic electron. Not all atoms are shaped this way, but a large number of them are. They connect with each other via electronic movement, kind of like how your hair stands up when you rub a balloon on your head. Not exactly the same thing, but this is an easy way to think about it.

These connections between atoms are what we call vibrations, and as we've already discussed, vibrations are the foundation of the Law of Attraction. Hopefully you've started to see how this is all connected.

We see this torus shape everywhere. It's the shape of the Earth's magnetic field. It's the shape of the energy field around the human heart. Even human DNA strands come in the form of a toroid shape, and the latest research shows that physicists have discovered a torus structure of energy that surrounds black holes.

It's everywhere, and it's based around the patterns of numbers, hence, we get vortex math.

Now, this is where things get interesting and tie into the image at the beginning of the chapter. Here it is again for reference.

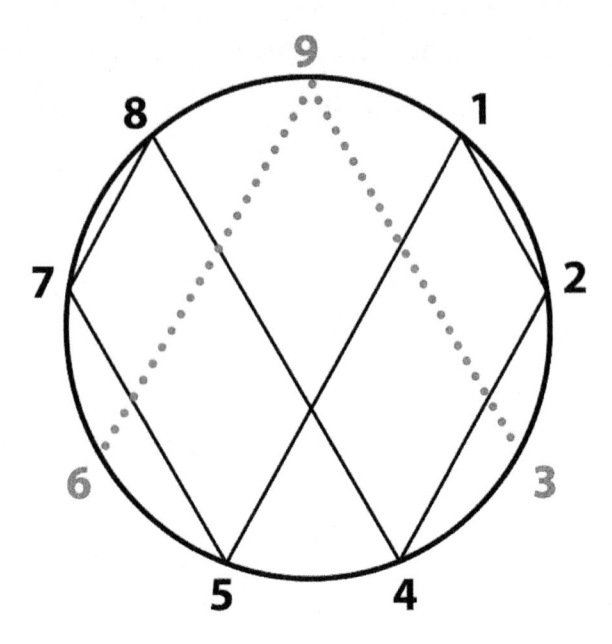

There's another common pattern that creates this pattern, and it goes as follows.

Start with 1, and double it for 2. Then double for 4. Double for 8. Double for 16, which we add together to get 7. Remember, we only use single-digit numbers because these nine numbers make up all numbers in existence.

16 doubled is 32, in which three plus two is five. 32 doubled is 64, added together to equal 10, which takes us back to one. This is an endless pattern that just goes on and on forever.

1, 2, 4, 8, 7, 5, and back to 1. See how they're when they're connected they create the vortex?

Even more interesting, the special numbers 3, 6, and 9 will never, ever come up. That's because these numbers are known as 'the ether.'

The Numbers of 3, 6, and 9

3, 6, and 9 are extraordinary numbers. The numbers of balance and manifestation. 3 and 6, for example, are known to represent yin and yang, which represents balance in the universe, the flow of energy in opposite directions. This is again the foundation of the Law of Attraction.

9 represents the discharge of energy into the universe. Again, I'll try and make this as simple as possible, but if numbers 1, 2, 4, 8, 7, 5, 1 represent everything in the material world, 3, 6, and 9 represent what we call the ether, or the non-material world.

That, of course, leaves zero, which represents the center point of everything, the center of the circle, which everything else is based around.

So, we have all the material numbers, we have 3 and 6, which represent what we can refer to as the non-material and the flow of energy between all that is material, then we have nine, which is related to three and six, but has its own unique take.

To many, nine represents the fingerprint of God. In the entirety of vortex math, nine is the most important number, which some call the number of the spirit. When we create a circle diagram representing vortex math, nine always goes at the top in the center. That's because of its importance.

This is known as the 'node,' signaling that it balances both sides of the circle and the vortex. This has been known throughout many religions worldwide, usually representing consciousness and enlightenment. In Hinduism, nine symbolizes perfection, divine, and completeness. This is the same in Egyptian culture, Chinese history, and even Norse mythology.

In the yin and yang symbol, 3 and 6 represent the left and the right side, whereas nine represents the line down the middle, bringing the two sides together.

This is why the numbers 3, 6, and 9 are so important. They are the numbers that represent all, a fundamental in the Law of Attraction, and that's exactly why the 369-manifestation method works.

How Does the 369 Method Work?

With all this talk of math and universal power, you might expect the 369 method to be a complicated series of processes that require multiple blackboards, a ton of chalk, and knowledge of complex equations or universal theory, but fortunately, that's not the case.

In fact, despite the complexity of vortex math, manifestation is incredibly simple no matter what method you use, and the 369 Method is no exception.

Like traditional manifestation, you'll take an affirmation or phrase that defines what you would like to manifest, and write it down. You'll write it down three times in the morning, six times during the day, and nine times in the evening.

For example, if you want to manifest more money into your life, you'll write, 'I am attracting wealth and abundance' three times in the morning, six times during the day, and nine times at night.

You can do this for as long as you like until you feel that the affirmation has sunk in and you've let it go. The general rule of thumb is to do it for 96 days, but some people like to do it for longer, and some people prefer to do it for shorter periods of time.

If you're just starting out, stick with the 96 days, and you'll get the full experience. That's exactly what the workbook attached to this book is for, and it's designed to help you achieve your dream in the easiest and most productive way.

When you start out, you'll notice changes in your life almost immediately. What seem like coincidences at first will start happening more often, and you'll start to feel like you're in the flow. Things will just start working out for you. And as you keep at it, these changes will become more pronounced and significant until they eventually manifest your desires.

It sounds so simple when you read it like this, but it's incredible to think how so many of us, myself included, go through our lives without ever truly tapping into this power. We get stuck in loops of petty thinking and quarrels with others. We get hung up on material objects that serve us no value, and we forget what it feels like to simply be happy.

I'm not saying that The 369 Method will magically make all of your problems disappear. But what I am saying is that if you commit to using this tool, and you use it with intention and purpose, it will help you raise your vibration so that you can attract the life you desire.

In other words, it will help you connect with the universal energy and tap into its limitless power.

And that, my friends, is true magic.

Chapter 3

Tuning into the Infinite

Everything we've spoken about so far has been leading up to this moment. In order to truly harness the power of manifestation, you need to be able to connect with the infinite.

And that's what this chapter is all about. At the core of everything lies the Law of Attraction. This is the most important thing to understand if you want to be successful in Manifestation.

So, what is the Law of Attraction?

The law of Attraction is the belief that people can bring positive or negative experiences into their lives by focusing on positive or negative thoughts. The basis of this theory is that like attracts like. So, if you want to attract more of something into your life, you must focus on that.

For example, if you want to attract more money into your life, you must focus on thoughts and feelings of abundance. If you're going to attract more love into your life, you need to focus on thoughts and feelings of love.

It's important to understand that the Law of Attraction doesn't just work with positive thoughts. It also works with negative thoughts. So, if you're focused on negative thoughts, you'll attract more negativity into your life.

This can be seen in every single area of your life. In my own life, I've always been 'bad' with money. At least, that's what I've always told myself. Whether I was looking at my overdrawn bank account, struggling to pay bills, or dreaming of saving for things in my life that I felt I was never going to get, I would constantly beat myself up because I was so bad at managing my money. It's what I always told myself.

However, by repeating these statements and letting myself go down the rabbit hole of thinking these thoughts, I was only attracting more financial instability into my life. I was sending out the energy that I was bad with money. Thus, this was the reality I manifested.

This is why it's so important to be aware of your thoughts and feelings because they are the things that will ultimately attract more of the same into your life.

The Law of Attraction is a powerful tool, but it's important to understand that it's not just about positive thinking. It's also about understanding your thoughts' role in your life and how they can either help or hinder the achievement of your goals.

This brings us into the art of visualization.

Visualization is the act of creating mental pictures of what you want to achieve. It's about using your imagination to see yourself in the future, achieving your goals, and living your dreams.

When you visualize something, you're planting a seed in your mind. This seed will grow and blossom into reality if you water it with positive thoughts, feelings, and emotions.

The more you visualize something, the more likely it is to happen. This is because you're sending out a strong message to the universe via the energy you create, saying that this is what you want. And as we know, like attracts like.

On the surface, this is something we all know and have heard repeatedly. Think happy thoughts, and you'll feel satisfied. Hold onto negative thoughts, and you'll become depressed. It's all about energy.

On a vibrational level, using Tesla's theories and research, when you think of a thought, and you visualize it in as much detail as possible, you're sending out a frequency. This frequency is then picked up by the universe and will start attracting things into your life that match that frequency.

The more you focus on something, the stronger the signal you're sending out becomes. And eventually, if you keep visualizing and thinking about something long enough, it will become your reality.

This is the best way to take control of your thoughts and feelings. Whereas a fleeting thought of how you feel about your life, your financial situation, or your relationships can have an effect before you notice it was even there, visualization is the intentional act of placing your focus on what you want.

And don't just take my word for it. Look at anyone in a successful position (however it is you define success), and you'll see the same logic used repeatedly, regardless of whether or not they attribute it to the Law of Attraction.

This happens over and over again. Celebrities talk about it all the time. Some of the biggest stars in the world have used the Law of Attraction to manifest their success. I've seen it in my life, whether it comes to writing books, earning enough money to pay my bills, or being in a relationship that actually serves me.

I spoke with a friend who shared her experiences not long ago. In her tween years, when she was doing her Bachelor's degree, she was working a job that took advantage of her and paid her next-to-nothing for the work she did. She booked a meeting with the manager, and for the next week, she wrote down on a sheet of paper, 'I will not accept anything other than a $5 per hour pay rise.'

A week passed, and after the meeting, the managers came back and said, "I'm sorry, we won't be able to offer anything more than a $5 pay rise. That's the best we can do."

She was shocked because that was exactly what she had wanted. She knew the Law of Attraction worked. But this was her first time using it, and she wanted to take it further.

A few years later, after she had graduated, she wanted to get a new job to set herself up while she sorted out her career path, just to pay the bills and help her get settled in the new city she had moved to with her partner. Understanding the power of the Law of Attraction, she told the universe she wanted a job that paid no less than $25 per hour.

This time, she went all out. She bought a cute, dedicated notebook for writing everything. She cut out magazine images of the things she wanted and stuck them in her book. This is where she also adopted the 369 method after reading about it online.

She wrote, "a job that pays no less than $25 per hour." Less than two weeks later, she got a call from a job she applied for saying they'll give her the position, and her pay would be $26 per hour.

You can go online and read stories in forums, chat rooms, and social media, where people share their experiences. Seriously, just go on TikTok or Instagram, search for the Law of Attraction hashtag, and see it for yourself. There are endless examples of people discovering this power for themselves each and every day.

You've undoubtedly seen the effects happen in your own life already. Perhaps you've had an idea for something, you dreamed of an event happening, or you had a vision (purposefully or otherwise), and then after some time, be it hours, days, weeks, months, or years, that vision came to life. That's the power of visualization and the Law of Attraction in full effect.

The list goes on, but the message is always the same: if you want to achieve something, visualize it happening.

What's more, if you can see it in your mind's eye, you have a higher chance of making it happen. All you need to do is take action and not give up until you achieve your goal.

The saying, 'fake it 'til you make it' embraces this same line of thinking. If you really try hard to put yourself where you want to be in life, literally acting as though you are where you want to be with the job you want, a bank account figure you're happy with, and surrounded by relationships that make you happy, before you know it, that life will be your reality.

Over time, the reality you dreamt of will be real.

And yes, I know what you're thinking. Everybody does. Surely this 'fake it 'til you make it approach' is too simple. Obviously if you're pretending in your head that you've got the job of your dreams, even if you don't right now, then you're just lying to yourself? Or if you pretend and act as though you're really confident when you're really not, then you'll only be creating the impression that you're confident, without actually being it.

Well, not exactly. It can feel like that at first, but this approach goes far deeper than this.

Let's say you want to be healthier.

You start visualizing yourself living a life where you're exercising and eating healthy. You decide what it means to be healthy, and you go through the motions acting out life as though you're a healthy person.

You shop for healthy foods and reduce snacking. You exercise everyday and drink lots of water. You go to the gym and meditate. Maybe even go to a few classes. You make sure you get enough sleep and you're turning off screens before bed, and so on. You start 'pretending' to be someone who's fit and healthy, and you do this every single day.

Sure, it feels like this isn't manifesting anything. On the surface this looks like you're just changing your life to be the person you want to be. Well, that's true. You are. But, it's actually so much more than this.

By making these decisions, you're controlling your own decisions, and you're placing your own energy where you want it to be.

This isn't manifesting, this is you working *internally*. You make decisions without your power to live the life you want to live. But, as you know, the vast majority of life happens to us, not from us. Our lives are affected by an infinite number of external factors.

The Law of Attraction works by providing you with opportunities from this external part of existence.

For example, while you're making proper decisions for yourself in the way of living a healthy life, you might receive a leaflet for a get-fit Bootcamp you'd love to join or an opportunity to join your local gym at a discounted price that fits your budget.

These are the 'coincidences' that you've perhaps noticed at many points in your life, but they are not coincidences at all. This is the power of the Law of Attraction in full effect.

Gratitude also plays a huge part in this.

Perhaps, paradoxically, you must be grateful for everything you have to gain new things and ways of living. This is because focusing on what you don't have, constantly striving for more, being jealous of what others have, and generally being discontent with your life sends a 'lack' vibration into the universe.

Because you're always wanting more, you never gain more because the energy you're sending into the universe says that you want to crave everything and anything that comes to mind. Because there's nothing in your life that's satisfying or fulfilling, you're always looking for the next thing, and you never get it.

On the other hand, if you focus on everything you have in your life and you're grateful for your current situation, you open yourself up to receiving more of what you want. You allow yourself to be content with what you have while also desiring more, and you send out a signal to the universe that says you're ready to receive.

When you focus on what you have, you open yourself up to receiving more.

This is the power of gratitude at work, and it's something that I've been working on lately.

I try to think of at least five things that I'm grateful for every day, no matter how small. This could be:

- The sun shining today

- My bed is comfortable

- My family and friends are supportive

- Having a job that I enjoy

By doing this, I'm not only gaining a greater sense of contentment in my life, but I'm also opening myself up to receiving more of what I want.

And that's the key to manifestation: being grateful for what you have while also desiring more and taking action towards your goals. It's not about changing your life or constantly moving in one direction. Instead, it's about living your life with intention and purpose and being open to the opportunities that the universe grants you.

All we're doing here is guiding the universe in the direction we want using the energy we're sending it.

Remember what I said before, we are all fragments of the universe and a way for the universe to experience itself. When you see a beautiful sunrise that takes your breath away, you're experiencing a part of yourself. You're both yourself and the sunset.

This can take a little while to wrap your head around, but it's the same idea behind the concept of being 'one' with each other and everything around. Like being 'one' with nature.

You're the trees, the bushes, the animals, and the air. We're all made up of the same things, particles and atoms that used to be other things before we were born, and will be other things after we're gone. It seems impossible because our human consciousness can only be conscious of the life we have, but the same star dust that makes you has been a part of someone else for millions of years.

Some of those atoms could have been other people, other animals, or even other planets.

We're all connected in this sense. Connected by everything. Connected by all energy. All the energy from the past, present, and the energy that will be. Because of this connection, and because the universe basically wants to have a good time and experience itself in the best possible way, it reacts to the energy you put out.

So, when you focus on what you want and send out that energy into the universe, the universe responds back, and thus the Law of Attraction is in effect.

With this in mind, let's continue our journey into how this works and some of the tools at your disposal. Next up, affirmations and manifestation. And don't worry if it feels like we've gone a little off-track from the 369 Method. This is all the theory behind the practice, so you know how it works. The 369 Method ties into all of these manifestation techniques, and this will become clear as we move through the book.

Chapter 4

Affirmation and Manifestation

Affirmations are another key part of the manifestation process. An affirmation is simply a statement that you repeat to yourself on a daily basis. This could be as simple as 'I am happy and healthy' or 'I am wealthy and abundant.'

The basic idea behind affirmations is that you program your subconscious mind to believe them by repeating these statements. As highlighted in the previous chapter, this is a way to transform the energy of your thoughts and feelings from being out of control and mindless. This is how most of us live, as I have done for many years. Thoughts come and go, all seemingly random and outside our control. But we can exert control over them.

This is what affirmations are for. By repeating these statements, especially in real-time, first-person format they're written in, they have real power to create real change, which is the core foundation of the 369 Method.

The truth is, you repeat affirmations to yourself every single day. If you look in the mirror and make a mental comment on how bad your skin has looked recently, that's an affirmation. If you look at your bank account and think about how bad you are at managing your money, that's an affirmation. Conversely, if you look in the mirror and think, 'I look fabulous today!' or 'I am great with money!' then those are, too.

The affirmations that we want to focus on are the ones that make us feel good, and help us manifest our desires into reality. So how do we go about doing this?

Well, the more you repeat an affirmation, the stronger the energy you're sending out. If you say something once and fleetingly, there's still an effect, but it's highly likely that nothing will happen.

If you repeat an affirmation daily, or even multiple times a day, this builds up energy and frequency, making it stronger, thus guiding the universe to take note of what you have to say. The stronger the energy you're sending out, the stronger the manifestation.

Repetition, in this sense, is the backbone of the 369 Method. You could go through life hoping to remember to repeat your affirmations as and when you remember them, but being the messy human beings most of us are, you're probably going to forget and fall out of the habit pretty soon.

Adopting a practice like the 369 Method gives you structure. You can make it part of your routine and work it into a habit that becomes an integral part of your day-to-day life. Therefore, you get into the flow state with it rather than feeling like you constantly have to remind yourself to do something.

We'll talk more about this when we get to the journaling section of this book, but for now, understand that affirmations and visualizations work together to help you envision what your dream life and goals can be, and guide you in the direction of manifesting that reality. By going through this process, you're sending out vibrational frequencies that come back to you, giving you what you want.

For now, however, here are some examples of affirmations you could use in your own practices, just to give you an idea and to get your creative juices flowing.

Health Affirmations

I am healthy and whole.

I am surrounded by an abundance of health and vitality.

I radiate health, wellness, and energy.

I am grateful for my strong and healthy body.

I listen to my body and give it what it needs.

My mind, body, and spirit are in perfect alignment.

Perfect health is my birthright.

I am open to, and receive, miracles of healing now.

I am grateful for my journey to perfect health and well-being.

My body is a temple of divine light and love.

Love Affirmations

I am worthy of love, respect, and affection.

I attract healthy and loving relationships into my life.

I am open to giving and receiving love.

I release any resentment, anger, or fear I have about love.

I am unconditional love.

I radiate love, kindness, and compassion in all that I do.

I attract my perfect soulmate/partner into my life.

I am grateful for the love in my life.

Love is always surrounding me.

I am a magnet for love.

All my relationships are healthy, supportive, and loving.

Money Affirmations

I am a money magnet.

I attract wealth and abundance into my life.

I am open to receiving all the good that life has to offer.

I am worthy of financial abundance.

I am grateful for my many blessings.

I release any and all blocks I have around money.

I am thankful for my abundant supply of money.

I am open to new and creative ways of making money.

My bank account is always growing.

Money comes to me easily and effortlessly.

Prosperity and abundance flow freely into my life.

Thank you, Universe!

Success Affirmations

I am successful in everything I do.

I attract success and abundance into my life.

I release any and all blocks I have around success.

I am open to new and creative ways of achieving success.

I am a success magnet.

Thank you, Universe!

Now, it's your turn! Write down some affirmations of your own and get ready to start manifesting your dream life!

Chapter 5

Self-Care and Manifestation

We're now at the final section of the theory part of this workbook, and this is a very important aspect of the manifestation process that many people miss. To some people I work with, it doesn't even cross their minds.

We hear it all the time, and Instagram is full of posts about it, but yes, self-care is essential, and it's something you need to be thinking about. I'm not going to list all the benefits of looking after yourself and what the science says. The internet is inundated with it, and you can look it up at your pleasure.

The basics are eating well, sleeping well, working hard, having downtime, socializing, getting enough sunlight, spending time in nature, and having balance. It's about looking after the physical, mental, emotional, and spiritual aspects of yourself. Yes, these are vital for a happy and healthy life, but what does it have to do with manifestation?

Well, actually everything.

You see, when you're taking care of yourself, you're raising your vibration. You're aligning yourself with what you want to attract into your life. When you have a high vibration, you're a match for what you desire, whether that's success, love, money, or anything else.

But it's not just about raising your vibration. It's also about being able to receive what you're trying to manifest.

You see, if you're working hard all the time and never taking a break, you're going to be too exhausted to notice the good things happening in your life, let alone take advantage of them.

But if you're taking care of yourself, you're going to be in a much better position to receive what you desire. You'll have the energy and enthusiasm to take action when opportunities present themselves, and you'll be able to enjoy the fruits of your manifestation.

The easiest way to think about this is; self-care is a way to show the universe that you're ready for the new manifestations you're working on. If you're not capable of looking after yourself now, you're not going to fare well if the new aspects of your life manifest.

Of course, you can work on manifesting certain aspects of your self-care practice, such as eating well or having a proper sleeping pattern, and that's fine. It's just as important to focus on the other areas of your life to ensure that you're doing everything you can to show the universe that you're capable of making the most of what you desire.

So, how can you integrate self-care into your manifestation practice?

Well, the first step is to understand that it's not just about taking baths and going for a walk-in a nearby park. It's about looking at all areas of your life and working out what you can do to start holistically caring for yourself.

For some people, that might mean quitting their job and finding something that better suits their lifestyle. For others, it might mean making time for themselves every day to do things they enjoy outside of work.

It's different for everyone, but the key is to be honest with yourself about what you need and what would make you happy. From there, it's just a matter of taking small daily steps to start changing your life.

Remember, self-care is an ongoing journey, not a one-time event. The more you do to take care of yourself, the better you'll feel and the better positioned you'll be to receive your manifestations.

As every chapter has so far, it all ties together. If you're looking after yourself to the best of your ability, affirming what you want in life, and actively being mindful and conscious of the thoughts and feelings you're having, journaling and meditating to strengthen your peace and ability to be self-aware, then you're setting yourself up for the strongest manifestation practice possible.

Chapter 6

Journaling Guide

And here we are, the part of the book where I hand over the reins to you. It's time to take control of your life and start using the 369 Method. This final chapter is pretty much a step-by-step guide on how to use the workbook for the next 96 days, highlighting everything you need to do and how it all works.

I've designed this workbook to be as easy to use as possible, but remember, manifestation is a personal practice and should be treated as such. If you want to mix things up and do things your way, or you have a certain kind of manifestation that you want to work on, feel free to use the workbook to follow your own path.

However, if you're just starting out or you want to address some of the most common obstacles and issues many of us face in the modern world, ultimately leading you to a solid place where you can actively and confidently start manifesting the life you want, then follow the outline and see the difference it makes in your day-to-day life.

So, without further ado, let's get into it.

Step #1 - Setting Up Your Workbook

First things first, set up your workbook.

This means getting it prepped and ready for you to write in. Placement is most important because you'll want to keep the book somewhere where you won't forget about it.

Personally, I found it very helpful to keep my book on my bedside table, so it was there when I woke up and went to bed (although I had to make a special effort to use it during the day), and I kept a pen with it at all times, so I had no excuse to get lazy and not to fill it out.

Which does happen. We're human, okay?

Step #2 - The 369 Method

Quite simply, the 369 Method runs for 96 days, or just over three months (3-6-9). Every single one of these 96 days, you'll find an affirmation that's specific to that day. Every day has a different one, but there are themes throughout the entire process that will help to build your confidence and will address issues that we all face at one time or another.

Included on each page, you'll see an affirmation that can help you get focused for the day and gives you a theme. Using this affirmation, you can create a manifestation that you want to manifest in your own life.

Of course, if you have your own ideas and there are any areas of your life you know you want to work on that don't fit the theme, that's fine. The point of this affirmation is to simply raise your vibration at the beginning of the day to get you into the mindset of manifesting the way you want to manifest.

There is an example in the workbook that I've filled out to show you what to do to get you started. However, once you find your own routine, you'll have no problems at all.

What is it that you want to manifest in your life? If you have a couple of things, take time to introspect and figure out what you want most in the list.

Once you've decided on what you need to manifest, you simply need to use the provided spaces to write it down three times in the morning, six times during the day, and nine times at night. You can write this down for as many days as you need to, until it manifests. Or, if the universe shows you a different path to your manifestation, adjust your words accordingly.

This repetition may seem too much, but it is building your vibration, drawing you closer to your manifestation, or to a divine realization of the action steps that will lead you to your manifestation.

As you write them down, I recommend actively saying them out loud, or at least saying them consciously and as clearly as possible in your mind to really have the best effect and the strongest manifestations.

Each day will also include a gratitude prompt so you can simply highlight one thing you're grateful for. You could note that you're thankful for a friend or coworker who's helped you out, or it could be about seeing the friendly cat on the street while you were heading home from work.

Just pop it in the space and try to tune into the feelings that come with putting it in writing. You'll notice your mindset shifting into a much more positive way of being, and you'll even start to notice yourself becoming more grateful for things throughout your day. This shift in the way you see the world is essential for manifestation and will help open up your ability to attract what you want into your life and send out all the positive energy you could ever want.

From here, you'll see the quote of the day. These quotes are related to the affirmation of the day and should help you to really think about what you're trying to manifest and how it applies to your life. This is just another little yet powerful way to help keep you focused on your goals and what you're working to achieve and ensure you're doing everything you need to do to bring about the strongest manifestations.

Finally, there's an added self-care prompt, which you can treat as a mini goal that you can focus on for just that day. Treat these as little nudges to help you stay focused on living your best life and as an opportunity to put a little extra effort into ensuring you're taking care of yourself. After all, if you want to be able to attract good things into your life, you've got to make sure you're taking care of the vessel that's going to help make it happen!

Step #3 - Live the 96 Days!

And that's it!

With just those three steps for the next 96 days, you'll begin to see some serious changes in yourself, your confidence, and how the Universe starts working with you instead of against you. I really can't wait to see how this works out for you, and I'll be here to support you every step of the way!

Conclusion

And with that, I'll leave you to it! The 369 Manifestation Journal is your key to unlocking the power of manifestation, and I have complete faith that if you commit to the practice, you'll see some amazing changes in your life.

Remember that this is a process, and you will have ups and downs. Some days will go amazingly, and some days, quite frankly, will suck. You're going to make mistakes, and you're going to miss days. Some days you just won't feel like it, whereas on others, you will feel so motivated you're going to wish you felt that way for the rest of your life.

It's the human experience, and it's something we all go through. The best thing you can do is be grateful for your good days and make the most of them. And when things get tough, just remember that they're not going to last forever and that you should just focus on doing the best you can with what you have, keep up with those little routines and habits that are going to lead to real, impactful, and significant changes in your life.

Conclusion

I'm so grateful that you've chosen to embark on this journey with me, and I can't wait to hear all about your successes. Let me know what you think via a review wherever you purchased your copy of this book as I will be reading them all, and I love to hear from you.

Wishing you all the best,

- **Layla**

PART TWO

JOURNAL

Here is an example of how your journal pages will look as you fill them out. In the blank spaces provided, feel free to write down your own affirmation, the self-care activity you indulged in that day, and what you're grateful for.

I wish you all the very best in your manifestation journey!

Harness The Power of The Universe   Date: /   /

I am on the right path.

☀

1. <u>I am filled with focus and dedication, ready to manifest my dream life</u>

2. <u>I am filled with focus and dedication, ready to manifest my dream life</u>

3. <u>I am filled with focus and dedication, ready to manifest my dream life</u>

☀

1. <u>I am filled with focus and dedication, ready to manifest my dream life</u>

2. <u>I am filled with focus and dedication, ready to manifest my dream life</u>

3. <u>I am filled with focus and dedication, ready to manifest my dream life</u>

4. <u>I am filled with focus and dedication, ready to manifest my dream life</u>

5. <u>I am filled with focus and dedication, ready to manifest my dream life</u>

6. <u>I am filled with focus and dedication, ready to manifest my dream life</u>

Self-Care

<u>Today I read five pages of the book I bought last month.</u>

_____

> *"The right path and easy path are usually two different things, and when it's time to choose, always choose the right path over the easy."*
> — *Deatri King-Bey*

🌙

1. I am filled with focus and dedication, ready to manifest my dream life
2. I am filled with focus and dedication, ready to manifest my dream life
3. I am filled with focus and dedication, ready to manifest my dream life
4. I am filled with focus and dedication, ready to manifest my dream life
5. I am filled with focus and dedication, ready to manifest my dream life
6. I am filled with focus and dedication, ready to manifest my dream life
7. I am filled with focus and dedication, ready to manifest my dream life
8. I am filled with focus and dedication, ready to manifest my dream life
9. I am filled with focus and dedication, ready to manifest my dream life

Today I'm grateful for

all the guidance the universe is always sending my way

Day 1 – 10

Building Your Self-Confidence

Harness The Power of The Universe   Date: /   /

I am on the right path.

1. _____
2. _____
3. _____

1. _____
2. _____
3. _____
4. _____
5. _____
6. _____

Self-Care

_____
_____

"The right path and easy path are usually two different things, and when it's time to choose, always choose the right path over the easy."
— *Deatri King-Bey*

1. _____
2. _____
3. _____
4. _____
5. _____
6. _____
7. _____
8. _____
9. _____

Today I'm grateful for

_____
_____

I am doing everything I can to achieve my goals.

1. _____
2. _____
3. _____

1. _____
2. _____
3. _____
4. _____
5. _____
6. _____

Self-Care

_____

_____

"Everyone's dream can come true if you just stick to it and work hard."

— Serena Williams

1. _____
2. _____
3. _____
4. _____
5. _____
6. _____
7. _____
8. _____
9. _____

Today I'm grateful for

_____

_____

I am taking action toward my dreams.

1. _____
2. _____
3. _____

1. _____
2. _____
3. _____
4. _____
5. _____
6. _____

Self-Care

_____

_____

"Dreams don't work unless you take action. The surest way to make your dreams come true is to live them."

— Roy T. Bennett

1. _____
2. _____
3. _____
4. _____
5. _____
6. _____
7. _____
8. _____
9. _____

Today I'm grateful for

_____

_____

Harness The Power of The Universe   *Date: / /*

I am in full control of my life.

1. _____
2. _____
3. _____

1. _____
2. _____
3. _____
4. _____
5. _____
6. _____

Self-Care

_____

_____

"You cannot control your circumstances, but you can control your character".

- Erwin Raphael McManus

1. _____

2. _____

3. _____

4. _____

5. _____

6. _____

7. _____

8. _____

9. _____

Today I'm grateful for

_____

_____

Harness The Power of The Universe   Date: /   /

I know that everything happens for a reason.

☀

1. _____

2. _____

3. _____

☀

1. _____

2. _____

3. _____

4. _____

5. _____

6. _____

Self-Care

_____

_____

"When life brings you full circle, pay attention. There's a lesson there."

— Mandy Hale

1. _____
2. _____
3. _____
4. _____
5. _____
6. _____
7. _____
8. _____
9. _____

Today I'm grateful for

_____

_____

Harness The Power of The Universe   Date: /   /

I release all fears and doubts about manifesting what I want.

1. _____
2. _____
3. _____

1. _____
2. _____
3. _____
4. _____
5. _____
6. _____

Self-Care

_____

_____

"Inaction breeds doubt and fear. Action breeds confidence and courage. If you want to conquer fear, do not sit at home and think about it. Go out and get busy."

- Dale Carnegie

☾

1. _____

2. _____

3. _____

4. _____

5. _____

6. _____

7. _____

8. _____

9. _____

Today I'm grateful for

_____

_____

Harness The Power of The Universe   Date: /   /

I am confident in myself and my ability to manifest my desires.

☀

1. _____

2. _____

3. _____

☀

1. _____

2. _____

3. _____

4. _____

5. _____

6. _____

Self-Care

_____

_____

"I think about trust and confidence as something that you earn every day, and we will keep at it, earning it every day."

- Lynn Good

🌙

1. _____
2. _____
3. _____
4. _____
5. _____
6. _____
7. _____
8. _____
9. _____

Today I'm grateful for

_____
_____

I am worthy of all my dreams and desires.

1. _____
2. _____
3. _____

1. _____
2. _____
3. _____
4. _____
5. _____
6. _____

Self-Care

_____

_____

"You are valuable because you exist. Not because of what you do or what you have done, but simply because you are."

— *Max Lucado*

🌙

1. _____
2. _____
3. _____
4. _____
5. _____
6. _____
7. _____
8. _____
9. _____

Today I'm grateful for

_____
_____

Harness The Power of The Universe					Date: / /

I am open to receiving what I want.

1. _____
2. _____
3. _____

1. _____
2. _____
3. _____
4. _____
5. _____
6. _____

Self-Care

_____

_____

"An open mind is not an end in itself, but a means to the end of finding truth."

- Peter Kreeft

🌙

1. _____
2. _____
3. _____
4. _____
5. _____
6. _____
7. _____
8. _____
9. _____

Today I'm grateful for

_____

_____

I show up for myself in every single moment.

1. _____
2. _____
3. _____

1. _____
2. _____
3. _____
4. _____
5. _____
6. _____

Self-Care

_____

_____

"Show up in every single moment like you're meant to be there."

- Unknown

1. _____
2. _____
3. _____
4. _____
5. _____
6. _____
7. _____
8. _____
9. _____

Today I'm grateful for

_____
_____
_____

Day 11 – 20

Manifesting Love, Romance, and Relationships

I attract love into my life.

1. _____
2. _____
3. _____

1. _____
2. _____
3. _____
4. _____
5. _____
6. _____

Self-Care

_____

_____

"Your task is not to seek love, but merely to seek and find all the barriers within yourself that you have built against it."

– Rumi

☾

1. _____
2. _____
3. _____
4. _____
5. _____
6. _____
7. _____
8. _____
9. _____

Today I'm grateful for

_____

_____

I release any fears or doubts about love.

1. _____
2. _____
3. _____

1. _____
2. _____
3. _____
4. _____
5. _____
6. _____

Self-Care

_____
_____

> *"I don't always make the best choices, but today I choose compassion over intolerance, sympathy over hatred and love over fear."*
>
> — *LJ Vanier*

☾

1. _____

2. _____

3. _____

4. _____

5. _____

6. _____

7. _____

8. _____

9. _____

Today I'm grateful for

_____

_____

Harness The Power of The Universe					Date: / /

I am open and receptive to love.

1. _____

2. _____

3. _____

1. _____

2. _____

3. _____

4. _____

5. _____

6. _____

Self-Care

_____

_____

"She always thought she needed someone to love when all she really needed to do was love the world and let love find her in its time and in its way"

– Kate McGahan

1. _____
2. _____
3. _____
4. _____
5. _____
6. _____
7. _____
8. _____
9. _____

Today I'm grateful for

_____
_____

I am confident in myself and my ability to attract a great relationship.

1. _____
2. _____
3. _____

1. _____
2. _____
3. _____
4. _____
5. _____
6. _____

Self-Care

_____

_____

"One day, someone will walk into your life and make you see why it never worked out with anyone else."

– Anonymous

1. _____
2. _____
3. _____
4. _____
5. _____
6. _____
7. _____
8. _____
9. _____

Today I'm grateful for

_____

_____

Harness The Power of The Universe					Date: / /

I deserve love and happiness.

1. _____

2. _____

3. _____

1. _____

2. _____

3. _____

4. _____

5. _____

6. _____

Self-Care

_____

_____

"Everything will change in your life when you finally learn that you deserve so much better."

- Karen Gibbs

☾

1. _____
2. _____
3. _____
4. _____
5. _____
6. _____
7. _____
8. _____
9. _____

Today I'm grateful for

_____
_____

Harness The Power of The Universe Date: / /

I am worthy of being loved.

1. _____

2. _____

3. _____

1. _____

2. _____

3. _____

4. _____

5. _____

6. _____

Self-Care

_____

_____

"We accept the love we think we deserve."

- Stephen Chbosky

1. _____
2. _____
3. _____
4. _____
5. _____
6. _____
7. _____
8. _____
9. _____

Today I'm grateful for

_____

_____

_____

Harness The Power of The Universe Date: /   /

I am lovable and deserving of love.

1. _____

2. _____

3. _____

1. _____

2. _____

3. _____

4. _____

5. _____

6. _____

Self-Care

_____

_____

"Love yourself and don't settle for less than what you deserve."

- Bethenny Frankel

1. _____
2. _____
3. _____
4. _____
5. _____
6. _____
7. _____
8. _____
9. _____

Today I'm grateful for

_____

_____

_____

I attract only healthy, positive, and loving relationships into my life.

1. _____
2. _____
3. _____

1. _____
2. _____
3. _____
4. _____
5. _____
6. _____

Self-Care

_____

_____

"A healthy relationship is a feast of affection/giving for both people; not one receiving crumbs and trying to convince themselves it's enough."

— Shannon Thomas

☾

1. _____
2. _____
3. _____
4. _____
5. _____
6. _____
7. _____
8. _____
9. _____

Today I'm grateful for

_____
_____

I release any resentment or bitterness I have towards love.

1. _____
2. _____
3. _____

1. _____
2. _____
3. _____
4. _____
5. _____
6. _____

Self-Care

_____

_____

> *"A healthy relationship will never require you to sacrifice your friends, your dreams, or your dignity."*
>
> *- Dinkar Kalotra*

🌙

1. _____
2. _____
3. _____
4. _____
5. _____
6. _____
7. _____
8. _____
9. _____

Today I'm grateful for

_____
_____

I am ready to receive love into my life.

1. _____
2. _____
3. _____

1. _____
2. _____
3. _____
4. _____
5. _____
6. _____

Self-Care

_____

_____

"Love is a fruit in season at all times, and within reach of every hand."

- Mother Teresa

🌙

1. _____

2. _____

3. _____

4. _____

5. _____

6. _____

7. _____

8. _____

9. _____

Today I'm grateful for

_____

_____

Day 21 – 30

Creating abundance in all areas of life

Harness The Power of The Universe Date: /   /

I am abundant in all areas of my life.

☀

1. _____

2. _____

3. _____

☀

1. _____

2. _____

3. _____

4. _____

5. _____

6. _____

Self-Care

_____

_____

"You are, at this moment, standing right in the middle of your own 'acres of diamonds.'"

- Earl Nightingale

🌙

1. _____
2. _____
3. _____
4. _____
5. _____
6. _____
7. _____
8. _____
9. _____

Today I'm grateful for

_____

_____

Date: / /

I have more than enough money to live a comfortable and happy life.

1. _____
2. _____
3. _____

1. _____
2. _____
3. _____
4. _____
5. _____
6. _____

Self-Care

_____
_____

"Money isn't important, but you have to have enough, so you don't have to think about it. Thinking about money is a drag."

- Jarvis Cocker

🌙

1. _____

2. _____

3. _____

4. _____

5. _____

6. _____

7. _____

8. _____

9. _____

Today I'm grateful for

_____

_____

Harness The Power of The Universe   Date: /   /

I attract wealth and abundance into my life.

1. _____
2. _____
3. _____

1. _____
2. _____
3. _____
4. _____
5. _____
6. _____

Self-Care

_____

_____

> *"We receive exactly what we see. See yourself living in abundance and you will attract it."*
>
> *– Rhonda Byrne*

1. _____
2. _____
3. _____
4. _____
5. _____
6. _____
7. _____
8. _____
9. _____

Today I'm grateful for

_____

_____

Harness The Power of The Universe   Date: /   /

I am confident and deserving of more money.

☀

1. _____
2. _____
3. _____

☀

1. _____
2. _____
3. _____
4. _____
5. _____
6. _____

Self-Care

_____

_____

"Financial fitness is not a pipe dream or a state of mind. It's a reality if you are willing to pursue it and embrace it."

–Will Robinson

🌙

1. _____
2. _____
3. _____
4. _____
5. _____
6. _____
7. _____
8. _____
9. _____

Today I'm grateful for

_____
_____

I am open to new and innovative ways of making money.

1. _____
2. _____
3. _____

1. _____
2. _____
3. _____
4. _____
5. _____
6. _____

Self-Care

_____

_____

> *"Truly wealthy people never worry about losing their money because they know that wherever money comes from there is an inexhaustible supply of it."*
>
> *– Deepak Chopra*

1. _____
2. _____
3. _____
4. _____
5. _____
6. _____
7. _____
8. _____
9. _____

Today I'm grateful for

_____

_____

I release any fears or doubts I have about money.

1. _____
2. _____
3. _____

1. _____
2. _____
3. _____
4. _____
5. _____
6. _____

Self-Care

_____

_____

"The better you feel about money, the more money you magnetize to yourself."

– Rhonda Byrne

1. _____
2. _____
3. _____
4. _____
5. _____
6. _____
7. _____
8. _____
9. _____

Today I'm grateful for

_____

_____

Harness The Power of The Universe   Date: / /

I know that I can always create more wealth if I need to.

☀

1. _____
2. _____
3. _____

☀

1. _____
2. _____
3. _____
4. _____
5. _____
6. _____

Self-Care

_____

_____

"Money is like blood; it must flow."

– Deepak Chopra

🌙

1. _____
2. _____
3. _____
4. _____
5. _____
6. _____
7. _____
8. _____
9. _____

Today I'm grateful for

_____
_____
_____

I am grateful for the abundance that I already have in my life.

1. _____
2. _____
3. _____

1. _____
2. _____
3. _____
4. _____
5. _____
6. _____

Self-Care

_____

_____

"The more you praise and celebrate your life, the more there is in life to celebrate."

– Oprah Winfrey

🌙

1. _____
2. _____
3. _____
4. _____
5. _____
6. _____
7. _____
8. _____
9. _____

Today I'm grateful for

_____

_____

I am willing to work hard to manifest more abundance into my life.

1.
2.
3.

1.
2.
3.
4.
5.
6.

Self-Care

"Ask for what you want and be prepared to get it."

– Maya Angelou

☾

1. _____
2. _____
3. _____
4. _____
5. _____
6. _____
7. _____
8. _____
9. _____

Today I'm grateful for

_____

_____

_____

I deserve to be wealthy and abundant.

1. _____
2. _____
3. _____

1. _____
2. _____
3. _____
4. _____
5. _____
6. _____

Self-Care

_____

_____

"There is nothing you cannot be, do, or have."

– Abraham Hicks

🌙

1. _____
2. _____
3. _____
4. _____
5. _____
6. _____
7. _____
8. _____
9. _____

Today I'm grateful for

_____

_____

_____

Day 31 – 40

Improving Your Health and Well-Being

I take care of my body, and it takes care of me.

1. _____

2. _____

3. _____

1. _____

2. _____

3. _____

4. _____

5. _____

6. _____

Self-Care

> *"Caring for your body, mind, and spirit is your greatest and grandest responsibility. It's about listening to the needs of your soul and then honoring them."*
>
> *- Kristi Ling*

1. _____
2. _____
3. _____
4. _____
5. _____
6. _____
7. _____
8. _____
9. _____

Today I'm grateful for

_____
_____

Harness The Power of The Universe　　　　　　　　　　Date:　　/　　/

I listen to my body and give it what it needs.

☀

1. _____
2. _____
3. _____

☀

1. _____
2. _____
3. _____
4. _____
5. _____
6. _____

Self-Care

_____

_____

"Your body is your best guide. It constantly tells you, in the form of pain or sensations, what's working for you and what's not."

— *Hina Hashmi*

🌙

1. _____
2. _____
3. _____
4. _____
5. _____
6. _____
7. _____
8. _____
9. _____

Today I'm grateful for

_____

_____

Harness The Power of The Universe Date: /   /

I am grateful for my health.

1. _____
2. _____
3. _____

1. _____
2. _____
3. _____
4. _____
5. _____
6. _____

Self-Care

"Good health and good sense are two of life's greatest blessings."

- Publilius Syrus

1. _____
2. _____
3. _____
4. _____
5. _____
6. _____
7. _____
8. _____
9. _____

Today I'm grateful for

_____
_____
_____

Harness The Power of The Universe   Date: /   /

I release any fears or doubts I have about my health.

1. _____
2. _____
3. _____

1. _____
2. _____
3. _____
4. _____
5. _____
6. _____

Self-Care

_____

_____

"No matter how much it gets abused, the body can restore balance. The first rule is to stop interfering with nature."

– Deepak Chopra

1. _____
2. _____
3. _____
4. _____
5. _____
6. _____
7. _____
8. _____
9. _____

Today I'm grateful for

_____

_____

Harness The Power of The Universe   Date: /   /

I take care of myself so that I can be the best version of myself.

☀

1. _____
2. _____
3. _____

☀

1. _____
2. _____
3. _____
4. _____
5. _____
6. _____

Self-Care

_____

_____

> *"Accept yourself, love yourself, and keep moving forward. If you want to fly, you have to give up what weighs you down."*
>
> — *Roy T. Bennett*

🌙

1. _____
2. _____
3. _____
4. _____
5. _____
6. _____
7. _____
8. _____
9. _____

Today I'm grateful for

_____
_____

Harness The Power of The Universe   Date: /   /

I am worth taking care of.

☀

1. _____
2. _____
3. _____

☀

1. _____
2. _____
3. _____
4. _____
5. _____
6. _____

Self-Care

_____

_____

"Be patient with yourself. Self-growth is tender; it's holy ground. There's no greater investment."

- Stephen Covey

☾

1. _____
2. _____
3. _____
4. _____
5. _____
6. _____
7. _____
8. _____
9. _____

Today I'm grateful for

_____

_____

Harness The Power of The Universe   Date: /   /

My health is important to me.

1. _____

2. _____

3. _____

1. _____

2. _____

3. _____

4. _____

5. _____

6. _____

Self-Care

_____

_____

"Physical fitness is the first requisite of happiness."

– Joseph Pilates

🌙

1. _____
2. _____
3. _____
4. _____
5. _____
6. _____
7. _____
8. _____
9. _____

Today I'm grateful for

_____
_____
_____

I make time for self-care every day.

☀

1. _____
2. _____
3. _____

☀

1. _____
2. _____
3. _____
4. _____
5. _____
6. _____

Self-Care

_____

_____

"Self-care is how you take your power back."

– Lalah Delia

1. _____
2. _____
3. _____
4. _____
5. _____
6. _____
7. _____
8. _____
9. _____

Today I'm grateful for

_____
_____
_____

Harness The Power of The Universe   Date: /   /

I eat healthy foods that nourish my body and make me feel good.

1. _____

2. _____

3. _____

1. _____

2. _____

3. _____

4. _____

5. _____

6. _____

Self-Care

_____

_____

"One cannot think well, love well, sleep well, if one has not dined well."

-Virginia Woolf

1. _____
2. _____
3. _____
4. _____
5. _____
6. _____
7. _____
8. _____
9. _____

Today I'm grateful for

_____

_____

Harness The Power of The Universe   Date: /   /

I am grateful for the ability to exercise and take care of my body.

1. _____
2. _____
3. _____

1. _____
2. _____
3. _____
4. _____
5. _____
6. _____

Self-Care

_____

_____

"If you don't make time for exercise, you'll probably have to make time for illness."

- Unknown

1. _____
2. _____
3. _____
4. _____
5. _____
6. _____
7. _____
8. _____
9. _____

Today I'm grateful for

_____

_____

Day 41 – 50

Developing Your Creativity

I am a creative person.

1. _____

2. _____

3. _____

1. _____

2. _____

3. _____

4. _____

5. _____

6. _____

Self-Care

_____

_____

"The creative adult is the child who survived."

- Ursula Leguin

1. _____
2. _____
3. _____
4. _____
5. _____
6. _____
7. _____
8. _____
9. _____

Today I'm grateful for

_____

_____

_____

Harness The Power of The Universe   Date: / /

I have many ideas and I express them in unique ways.

1. _____

2. _____

3. _____

1. _____

2. _____

3. _____

4. _____

5. _____

6. _____

Self-Care

_____

_____

"The desire to create is one of the deepest yearnings of the human soul."

- Dieter F. Uchtdorf

🌙

1. _____
2. _____
3. _____
4. _____
5. _____
6. _____
7. _____
8. _____
9. _____

Today I'm grateful for

_____

_____

I am confident in my creativity and I use it to its fullest potential.

☀

1. _____
2. _____
3. _____

☀

1. _____
2. _____
3. _____
4. _____
5. _____
6. _____

Self-Care

_____

_____

"Creativity is seeing what others see and thinking what no one else ever thought."

- Albert Einstein

1. _____
2. _____
3. _____
4. _____
5. _____
6. _____
7. _____
8. _____
9. _____

Today I'm grateful for

_____

_____

Harness The Power of The Universe   Date: /   /

I enjoy being creative and exploring new things.

☀

1. _____

2. _____

3. _____

☀

1. _____

2. _____

3. _____

4. _____

5. _____

6. _____

Self-Care

_____

_____

"Creativity is inventing, experimenting, growing, taking risks, breaking rules, making mistakes, and having fun."

- Mary Lou Cook

1. _____
2. _____
3. _____
4. _____
5. _____
6. _____
7. _____
8. _____
9. _____

Today I'm grateful for

_____

_____

Harness The Power of The Universe   Date: /   /

I am open to new ideas and ways of expressing myself.

1. _____
2. _____
3. _____

1. _____
2. _____
3. _____
4. _____
5. _____
6. _____

Self-Care

_____

_____

"There is no doubt that creativity is the most important human resource of all. Without creativity, there would be no progress, and we would be forever repeating the same patterns."

- Edward De Bono

🌙

1. _____
2. _____
3. _____
4. _____
5. _____
6. _____
7. _____
8. _____
9. _____

Today I'm grateful for

_____

_____

Harness The Power of The Universe   Date: /   /

I release any fears or doubts I have about being creative.

☀

1. _____
2. _____
3. _____

☀

1. _____
2. _____
3. _____
4. _____
5. _____
6. _____

Self-Care

_____

_____

> *"A creative life is an amplified life. It's a bigger life, a happier life, an expanded life, and a hell of a lot more interesting life"*
>
> *- Elizabeth Gilbert*

1. _____
2. _____
3. _____
4. _____
5. _____
6. _____
7. _____
8. _____
9. _____

Today I'm grateful for

_____

_____

I know that my creativity is one of my strengths.

1. _____
2. _____
3. _____

1. _____
2. _____
3. _____
4. _____
5. _____
6. _____

Self-Care

_____
_____

"An essential aspect of creativity is not being afraid to fail".

- Edwin Land

🌙

1. _____
2. _____
3. _____
4. _____
5. _____
6. _____
7. _____
8. _____
9. _____

Today I'm grateful for

_____
_____
_____

Harness The Power of The Universe		Date: / /

I use my creativity to make my life more enjoyable.

1. _____
2. _____
3. _____

1. _____
2. _____
3. _____
4. _____
5. _____
6. _____

Self-Care

_____

_____

"Creativity is intelligence having fun."

- Albert Einstein

🌙

1. _____
2. _____
3. _____
4. _____
5. _____
6. _____
7. _____
8. _____
9. _____

Today I'm grateful for

_____

_____

_____

Harness The Power of The Universe   Date: /   /

I am grateful for my creative talent.

1. _____
2. _____
3. _____

1. _____
2. _____
3. _____
4. _____
5. _____
6. _____

Self-Care

_____

_____

"The comfort zone is the great enemy to creativity."

- Dan Stevens

🌙

1. _____
2. _____
3. _____
4. _____
5. _____
6. _____
7. _____
8. _____
9. _____

Today I'm grateful for

_____
_____
_____

Harness The Power of The Universe   Date: /   /

I express my creativity every day.

☀

1. _____
2. _____
3. _____

☀

1. _____
2. _____
3. _____
4. _____
5. _____
6. _____

Self-Care

_____

_____

"Don't wait for inspiration. It comes while working."

- Henri Matisse

1. _____
2. _____
3. _____
4. _____
5. _____
6. _____
7. _____
8. _____
9. _____

Today I'm grateful for

_____
_____
_____

Day 51 – 60

Achieving Your Goals and Dreams

Harness The Power of The Universe   Date: /   /

I am capable of achieving all my goals and dreams.

1. _____

2. _____

3. _____

1. _____

2. _____

3. _____

4. _____

5. _____

6. _____

Self-Care

_____

_____

"You are capable of more than you know. Choose a goal that seems right for you and strive to be the best, however hard the path. Aim high. Behave honorably. Prepare to be alone at times, and to endure failure. Persist! The world needs all you can give."

- E. O. Wilson

1. _____
2. _____
3. _____
4. _____
5. _____
6. _____
7. _____
8. _____
9. _____

Today I'm grateful for

_____

_____

I take action towards my goals every day.

1. _____
2. _____
3. _____

1. _____
2. _____
3. _____
4. _____
5. _____
6. _____

Self-Care

_____

_____

"Action is the antidote to despair."

— Joan Baez

1. _____

2. _____

3. _____

4. _____

5. _____

6. _____

7. _____

8. _____

9. _____

Today I'm grateful for

_____

_____

_____

Harness The Power of The Universe Date: /   /

I am confident and deserving of achieving my goals.

☀

1. _____

2. _____

3. _____

☀

1. _____

2. _____

3. _____

4. _____

5. _____

6. _____

Self-Care

_____

_____

"The minute you settle for less than you deserve, you get even less than you settled for."

- Maureen Dowd

🌙

1. _____

2. _____

3. _____

4. _____

5. _____

6. _____

7. _____

8. _____

9. _____

Today I'm grateful for

_____

_____

Harness The Power of The Universe

I release any fears or doubts I have about achieving my goals.

1. _____
2. _____
3. _____

1. _____
2. _____
3. _____
4. _____
5. _____
6. _____

Self-Care

> *"Procrastination is the fear of success. People procrastinate because they are afraid of the success that they know will result if they move ahead now. Because success is heavy, carries a responsibility with it, it is much easier to procrastinate and live on the 'someday I'll' philosophy."*
>
> *- Denis Waitley*

1. _____
2. _____
3. _____
4. _____
5. _____
6. _____
7. _____
8. _____
9. _____

Today I'm grateful for

_____

_____

Harness The Power of The Universe					Date: / /

I know that if I work hard, anything is possible.

1. _____

2. _____

3. _____

1. _____

2. _____

3. _____

4. _____

5. _____

6. _____

Self-Care

_____

_____

"Without hard work, nothing grows but weeds."

- Gordon B. Hinckley

1. _____
2. _____
3. _____
4. _____
5. _____
6. _____
7. _____
8. _____
9. _____

Today I'm grateful for

_____

_____

_____

Harness The Power of The Universe   Date: / /

I am willing to put in the effort to achieve my goals.

1. _____
2. _____
3. _____

1. _____
2. _____
3. _____
4. _____
5. _____
6. _____

Self-Care

_____

_____

"Happiness is the real sense of fulfillment that comes from hard work."

- Joseph Barbara

1. _____
2. _____
3. _____
4. _____
5. _____
6. _____
7. _____
8. _____
9. _____

Today I'm grateful for

_____

_____

I deserve to achieve all my goals and dreams.

1. _____

2. _____

3. _____

1. _____

2. _____

3. _____

4. _____

5. _____

6. _____

Self-Care

_____

_____

"We only get what we believe that we deserve. Raise the bar, raise your standards, and you will receive a better outcome."

- Joel Brown

🌙

1. _____
2. _____
3. _____
4. _____
5. _____
6. _____
7. _____
8. _____
9. _____

Today I'm grateful for

_____

_____

Harness The Power of The Universe   Date: /   /

I am grateful for the progress I have made.

1. _____

2. _____

3. _____

1. _____

2. _____

3. _____

4. _____

5. _____

6. _____

Self-Care

_____

_____

"Remember how far you've come, not just how far you have to go. You are not where you want to be, but neither are you where you used to be."

-Rick Warren

🌙

1. _____
2. _____
3. _____
4. _____
5. _____
6. _____
7. _____
8. _____
9. _____

Today I'm grateful for

_____

_____

Harness The Power of The Universe   Date: /   /

I am excited to achieve all my goals and dreams.

☀

1. _____

2. _____

3. _____

☀

1. _____

2. _____

3. _____

4. _____

5. _____

6. _____

Self-Care

_____

_____

"There is no passion to be found in settling for a life that is less than the one you are capable of living."

- Nelson Mandela

1. _____
2. _____
3. _____
4. _____
5. _____
6. _____
7. _____
8. _____
9. _____

Today I'm grateful for

_____

_____

Day 61 – 70

Manifesting Your Ideal Career or Job

I attract my ideal career or job into my life.

1. _____
2. _____
3. _____

1. _____
2. _____
3. _____
4. _____
5. _____
6. _____

Self-Care

_____
_____

> *"The only way to do great work is to love what you do. If you haven't found it yet, keep looking. Don't settle."*
>
> *— Steve Jobs*

🌙

1. _____
2. _____
3. _____
4. _____
5. _____
6. _____
7. _____
8. _____
9. _____

Today I'm grateful for

_____
_____

Harness The Power of The Universe   Date: /   /

I release any fears or doubts I have about finding my dream job.

1. _____
2. _____
3. _____

1. _____
2. _____
3. _____
4. _____
5. _____
6. _____

Self-Care

_____
_____

"You gain strength, courage, and confidence by every experience in which you really stop to look fear in the face. You are able to say to yourself, 'I have lived through this horror. I can take the next thing that comes along.' You must do the thing you think you cannot do."

- Eleanor Roosevelt

1. _____
2. _____
3. _____
4. _____
5. _____
6. _____
7. _____
8. _____
9. _____

Today I'm grateful for

_____
_____

I am confident in my ability to find a career or job that I love.

1. _____

2. _____

3. _____

1. _____

2. _____

3. _____

4. _____

5. _____

6. _____

Self-Care

_____

_____

"You can only become truly accomplished at something you love. Don't make money your goal. Instead pursue the things you love doing and then do them so well that people can't take their eyes off of you."

- Maya Angelou

🌙

1. _____

2. _____

3. _____

4. _____

5. _____

6. _____

7. _____

8. _____

9. _____

Today I'm grateful for

_____

_____

I am open to new opportunities.

1. _____
2. _____
3. _____

1. _____
2. _____
3. _____
4. _____
5. _____
6. _____

Self-Care

_____

_____

"There is no passion to be found in playing small — in settling for a life that is less than you are capable of living."

—Nelson Mandela

☾

1. _____
2. _____
3. _____
4. _____
5. _____
6. _____
7. _____
8. _____
9. _____

Today I'm grateful for

_____

_____

I release any resentment or bitterness I have towards my current or past jobs.

1. _____
2. _____
3. _____

1. _____
2. _____
3. _____
4. _____
5. _____
6. _____

Self-Care

_____

_____

"Let go of the past, but keep the lessons it taught you."

–Chiara Gizzi

🌙

1. _____
2. _____
3. _____
4. _____
5. _____
6. _____
7. _____
8. _____
9. _____

Today I'm grateful for

_____

_____

_____

Harness The Power of The Universe   Date: /   /

My experiences lead me to my dream job.

1. _____

2. _____

3. _____

1. _____

2. _____

3. _____

4. _____

5. _____

6. _____

Self-Care

_____

_____

"I've missed more than 9,000 shots in my career. I've lost almost 300 games. 26 times, I've been trusted to take the game winning shot and missed. I've failed over and over and over again in my life. And that is why I succeed."

—*Michael Jordan*

1. _____
2. _____
3. _____
4. _____
5. _____
6. _____
7. _____
8. _____
9. _____

Today I'm grateful for

_____
_____

I am grateful for the lessons I have learned from my past experiences.

1. _____
2. _____
3. _____

1. _____
2. _____
3. _____
4. _____
5. _____
6. _____

Self-Care

_____

_____

"Without making mistakes, there won't be lessons learned. Without getting hurt, there won't be knowledge gained. The only way we grow is by learning from the past. Always be willing to learn and grow daily."

- Kemi Sogunle

1. _____
2. _____
3. _____
4. _____
5. _____
6. _____
7. _____
8. _____
9. _____

Today I'm grateful for

_____
_____

I am excited to find my dream job or career.

1. _____

2. _____

3. _____

1. _____

2. _____

3. _____

4. _____

5. _____

6. _____

Self-Care

_____

_____

"The future belongs to those who believe in the beauty of their dreams."

- Eleanor Roosevelt

1. _____
2. _____
3. _____
4. _____
5. _____
6. _____
7. _____
8. _____
9. _____

Today I'm grateful for

_____
_____

Harness The Power of The Universe   Date: /   /

I deserve to love my job and be successful in it.

1. _____

2. _____

3. _____

1. _____

2. _____

3. _____

4. _____

5. _____

6. _____

Self-Care

_____

_____

> *"It's not what you achieve, it's what you overcome. That's what defines your career."*
>
> *– Carlton Fisk*

1. _____
2. _____
3. _____
4. _____
5. _____
6. _____
7. _____
8. _____
9. _____

Today I'm grateful for

_____

_____

Day 71 – 80

Creating a Life You Love

Harness The Power of The Universe   Date: /   /

I love my life.

☀

1. _____
2. _____
3. _____

☀

1. _____
2. _____
3. _____
4. _____
5. _____
6. _____

Self-Care

_____

_____

"Be yourself; everyone else is already taken."

—*Oscar Wilde*

🌙

1. _____
2. _____
3. _____
4. _____
5. _____
6. _____
7. _____
8. _____
9. _____

Today I'm grateful for

_____

_____

_____

Harness The Power of The Universe   Date: /   /

I am grateful for all of the wonderful things in my life.

1. _____

2. _____

3. _____

1. _____

2. _____

3. _____

4. _____

5. _____

6. _____

Self-Care

_____

_____

"We learned about gratitude and humility - that so many people had a hand in our success."

- Michelle Obama

1. _____
2. _____
3. _____
4. _____
5. _____
6. _____
7. _____
8. _____
9. _____

Today I'm grateful for

_____

_____

Harness The Power of The Universe   Date: /   /

I attract only positive and good things into my life.

☀

1. _____

2. _____

3. _____

☀

1. _____

2. _____

3. _____

4. _____

5. _____

6. _____

Self-Care

_____

_____

"If you are depressed you are living in the past. If you are anxious you're living in the future. If you are at peace you are living in the present."

– Lao Tzu

1. _____
2. _____
3. _____
4. _____
5. _____
6. _____
7. _____
8. _____
9. _____

Today I'm grateful for

_____
_____

Harness The Power of The Universe   Date: /   /

I release any negative thoughts or emotions I have about my life.

☀

1. _____

2. _____

3. _____

☀

1. _____

2. _____

3. _____

4. _____

5. _____

6. _____

Self-Care

_____

_____

> *"Shout out to everyone transcending a mindset, mentality, desire, belief, emotion, habit, behavior or vibration, that no longer serves them."*
>
> — *Lalah Delia*

1. _____
2. _____
3. _____
4. _____
5. _____
6. _____
7. _____
8. _____
9. _____

Today I'm grateful for

_____

_____

I know that I am in control of my own happiness.

1. _____
2. _____
3. _____

1. _____
2. _____
3. _____
4. _____
5. _____
6. _____

Self-Care

_____

_____

"Happiness is when what you think, what you say, and what you do are in harmony."

—*Mahatma Gandhi*

☾

1. _____
2. _____
3. _____
4. _____
5. _____
6. _____
7. _____
8. _____
9. _____

Today I'm grateful for

_____
_____

Harness The Power of The Universe — Date: /   /

I make choices that lead me towards a life I love.

☀

1. _____
2. _____
3. _____

☀

1. _____
2. _____
3. _____
4. _____
5. _____
6. _____

Self-Care

_____
_____

"Every morning you have two choices: Continue to sleep with your dreams or wake up and chase your dreams. The choice is yours."

- Unknown

☾

1. _____
2. _____
3. _____
4. _____
5. _____
6. _____
7. _____
8. _____
9. _____

Today I'm grateful for

_____

_____

Harness The Power of The Universe   Date: /   /

I take action steps every day to create a life I love.

☀

1. _____

2. _____

3. _____

☀

1. _____

2. _____

3. _____

4. _____

5. _____

6. _____

Self-Care

_____

_____

"The best time to plant a tree is twenty years ago. The second-best time is today."

– Chinese Proverb

🌙

1. _____
2. _____
3. _____
4. _____
5. _____
6. _____
7. _____
8. _____
9. _____

Today I'm grateful for

_____

_____

Harness The Power of The Universe   Date: /   /

I am excited about my life and everything it has to offer.

1. _____

2. _____

3. _____

1. _____

2. _____

3. _____

4. _____

5. _____

6. _____

Self-Care

_____

_____

"You only live once, but if you do it right, once is enough."

— *Mae West*

🌙

1. _____
2. _____
3. _____
4. _____
5. _____
6. _____
7. _____
8. _____
9. _____

Today I'm grateful for

_____
_____
_____

Harness The Power of The Universe   Date: /   /

I deserve to have a life that I love.

1. _____

2. _____

3. _____

1. _____

2. _____

3. _____

4. _____

5. _____

6. _____

Self-Care

_____

_____

"If you don't know what you want, you'll never find it. If you don't know what you deserve, you'll always settle for less. You will wander aimlessly, uncomfortably numb in your comfort zone, wondering how life has ended up here. Life starts now, live, love, laugh, and let your light shine!"

— Rob Liano

🌙

1. _____

2. _____

3. _____

4. _____

5. _____

6. _____

7. _____

8. _____

9. _____

Today I'm grateful for

_____

_____

Harness The Power of The Universe   Date: /   /

I am grateful for the progress I have made.

1. _____

2. _____

3. _____

1. _____

2. _____

3. _____

4. _____

5. _____

6. _____

Self-Care

_____

_____

> *"Love yourself a little extra right now. You're evolving, learning, healing, growing, and discovering yourself all at once. It's about to get magical for you."*
>
> *- Idil Ahmed*

1. _____
2. _____
3. _____
4. _____
5. _____
6. _____
7. _____
8. _____
9. _____

Today I'm grateful for

_____

_____

Day 81 – 90

Forgiving Yourself and Others

Harness The Power of The Universe   Date: /   /

I forgive myself for any mistakes I have made in the past.

☀

1. _____

2. _____

3. _____

☀

1. _____

2. _____

3. _____

4. _____

5. _____

6. _____

Self-Care

_____

_____

"Always forgive, but never forget. Learn from your mistakes, but never regret."

- Unknown

1. _____
2. _____
3. _____
4. _____
5. _____
6. _____
7. _____
8. _____
9. _____

Today I'm grateful for

_____

_____

I release any negative emotions I have towards myself.

1. _____

2. _____

3. _____

1. _____

2. _____

3. _____

4. _____

5. _____

6. _____

Self-Care

_____

_____

> *"Don't dwell on what went wrong. Instead, focus on what to do next. Spend your energy moving forward together towards an answer."*
>
> *– Denis Waitley*

🌙

1. _____
2. _____
3. _____
4. _____
5. _____
6. _____
7. _____
8. _____
9. _____

Today I'm grateful for

_____

_____

I am worthy of forgiveness and compassion.

1. _____
2. _____
3. _____

1. _____
2. _____
3. _____
4. _____
5. _____
6. _____

Self-Care

_____

_____

"Love yourself, accept yourself, forgive yourself and be good to yourself, because without you the rest of us are without a source of many wonderful things."

— *Leo F. Buscaglia*

1. _____
2. _____
3. _____
4. _____
5. _____
6. _____
7. _____
8. _____
9. _____

Today I'm grateful for

_____

_____

Harness The Power of The Universe Date: /   /

I forgive others for any hurt they have caused me.

☀

1. _____
2. _____
3. _____

☀

1. _____
2. _____
3. _____
4. _____
5. _____
6. _____

Self-Care

_____

_____

"To forgive is the highest, most beautiful form of love. In return, you will receive untold peace and happiness."

- Robert Muller

1. _____
2. _____
3. _____
4. _____
5. _____
6. _____
7. _____
8. _____
9. _____

Today I'm grateful for

_____

_____

Harness The Power of The Universe Date: /   /

I release any resentment or bitterness I have towards others.

1. _____
2. _____
3. _____

1. _____
2. _____
3. _____
4. _____
5. _____
6. _____

Self-Care

_____

_____

"Forgiveness is a sign that the person who has wronged you means more to you than the wrong they have dealt."

- Ben Greenhalgh

1. _____
2. _____
3. _____
4. _____
5. _____
6. _____
7. _____
8. _____
9. _____

Today I'm grateful for

_____

_____

Harness The Power of The Universe　　　　　　　　Date:　 /　 /

I know that everyone is doing the best they can with what they have.

☀

1. _____
2. _____
3. _____

☀

1. _____
2. _____
3. _____
4. _____
5. _____
6. _____

Self-Care

_____
_____

"Let us forgive each other – only then will we live in peace."

- Leo Nikolaevich Tolstoy

☾

1. _____
2. _____
3. _____
4. _____
5. _____
6. _____
7. _____
8. _____
9. _____

Today I'm grateful for

_____

_____

_____

I am grateful for the lessons I have learned from my past experiences.

1. _____
2. _____
3. _____

1. _____
2. _____
3. _____
4. _____
5. _____
6. _____

Self-Care

_____

_____

> *"Gratitude is a powerful catalyst for happiness. It's the spark that lights a fire of joy in your soul."*
>
> *– Amy Collette*

🌙

1. _____
2. _____
3. _____
4. _____
5. _____
6. _____
7. _____
8. _____
9. _____

Today I'm grateful for

_____

_____

I am open to forgiving others and myself.

1. _____
2. _____
3. _____

1. _____
2. _____
3. _____
4. _____
5. _____
6. _____

Self-Care

_____

_____

> "*The act of forgiveness takes place in our own mind. It really has nothing to do with the other person.*"
>
> *- Louise Hay*

🌙

1. _____
2. _____
3. _____
4. _____
5. _____
6. _____
7. _____
8. _____
9. _____

Today I'm grateful for

_____

_____

Harness The Power of The Universe   Date: /   /

I deserve to live a life free of resentment and bitterness.

☀

1. _____

2. _____

3. _____

☀

1. _____

2. _____

3. _____

4. _____

5. _____

6. _____

Self-Care

_____

_____

"Worry, hate, fear - together with their offshoots: anxiety, bitterness, impatience, avarice, unkindness, judgmentalness, and condemnation - all attack the body at the cellular level. It is impossible to have a healthy body under these conditions."

— *Neale Donald Walsch*

1. _____
2. _____
3. _____
4. _____
5. _____
6. _____
7. _____
8. _____
9. _____

Today I'm grateful for

_____

_____

Harness The Power of The Universe   Date: / /

Forgiveness is liberating.

1. _____
2. _____
3. _____

1. _____
2. _____
3. _____
4. _____
5. _____
6. _____

Self-Care

_____

_____

"Bitterness kills the soul."

— *Anthony Ray Hinton*

1. _____
2. _____
3. _____
4. _____
5. _____
6. _____
7. _____
8. _____
9. _____

Today I'm grateful for

_____
_____
_____

Day 91 – 96

Manifest Your Reality

Harness The Power of The Universe   Date: /   /

I am in control of my reality.

1. _____

2. _____

3. _____

1. _____

2. _____

3. _____

4. _____

5. _____

6. _____

Self-Care

_____

_____

"No one has power over you unless you give it to them, you are in control of your life and your choices decide your own fate."

- Anonymous

☾

1. _____
2. _____
3. _____
4. _____
5. _____
6. _____
7. _____
8. _____
9. _____

Today I'm grateful for

_____

_____

I create my own reality with my thoughts, emotions, and actions.

☀

1. _____

2. _____

3. _____

☀

1. _____

2. _____

3. _____

4. _____

5. _____

6. _____

Self-Care

_____

_____

"Don't become a prisoner of your own reality, set yourself free by creating a life worth living."

- Steven Redhead

1. _____
2. _____
3. _____
4. _____
5. _____
6. _____
7. _____
8. _____
9. _____

Today I'm grateful for

_____

_____

I am deserving of a life that I love.

1. _____
2. _____
3. _____

1. _____
2. _____
3. _____
4. _____
5. _____
6. _____

Self-Care

_____

_____

"Stop blaming everybody and everything for what's going on. If you really believe that you deserve better, then you would have it."

- Bobby Williams

🌙

1. _____

2. _____

3. _____

4. _____

5. _____

6. _____

7. _____

8. _____

9. _____

Today I'm grateful for

_____

_____

I attract what I focus on.

1. _____
2. _____
3. _____

1. _____
2. _____
3. _____
4. _____
5. _____
6. _____

Self-Care

"Once you make a decision, the universe conspires to make it happen."

– Ralph Waldo Emerson

1. _____
2. _____
3. _____
4. _____
5. _____
6. _____
7. _____
8. _____
9. _____

Today I'm grateful for

_____
_____

I take action steps every day to manifest my dream life.

☀

1. _____
2. _____
3. _____

☀

1. _____
2. _____
3. _____
4. _____
5. _____
6. _____

Self-Care

_____

_____

"It's our intention. Our intention is everything. Nothing happens on this planet without it. Not one single thing has ever been accomplished without intention."

—Jim Carrey

1. _____
2. _____
3. _____
4. _____
5. _____
6. _____
7. _____
8. _____
9. _____

Today I'm grateful for

_____

_____

Harness The Power of The Universe   Date: /   /

Everything is possible for me.

1. _____
2. _____
3. _____

1. _____
2. _____
3. _____
4. _____
5. _____
6. _____

Self-Care

_____

_____

"You create your thoughts, your thoughts create your intentions, and your intentions create your reality."

—*Dr. Wayne Dyer*

1. _____
2. _____
3. _____
4. _____
5. _____
6. _____
7. _____
8. _____
9. _____

Today I'm grateful for

_____

_____